Things
I Didn't Know
I Loved

Things
I Didn't Know
I Loved

poems

Tim Nolan

NODIN PRESS

Copyright © 2024 by Tim Nolan, all rights reserved. For permission to reproduce selections from this book or to learn more about Nodin Press, visit www.nodinpress.com.

Cover: John Toren

ISBN: 978-1-947237-61-2

Library of Congress Control Number: 2024946469

Published by

Nodin Press
210 Edge Place
Minneapolis, MN 55418
www.nodinpress.com

Printed in U.S.A.

For Kate, Lizzie, Maeve & Frank

Contents

I

Sunlight Through the Open Window | 13
Because | 14
Strange | 15
My Blue Socks | 16
These Strange Times | 17
Cars on the Freeway | 18
If I Get This Wrong | 19
Sketches | 20
Lincoln | 21
My Mother's Babies | 22
You Told Us | 24
Brooklyn Bridge | 25
Trumpet | 26
One October Night | 27
1957 | 28
My First Poems | 29

II

Us | 33
My Parents' Wedding Album |34
This | 35
With Adam Zagajewski | 36
All of Us | 37
Songs | 38
Maria Callas | 39
A Train South | 40
I Remember When My Mother Cried | 41

121 East 88th Street | 42
Geese on the Highway | 44
Minnehaha Creek, 1969 | 45
Steelhead Trout | 47
Morton Man Dies in ATV Crash in
Renville County | 48
Oyster Shells | 49

III

I Like Room Service | 53
When | 54
Scam Likely | 55
The Sweetness of Water | 56
For Where You Used to Live | 57
Aramaic Galilean Accent | 58
Crickets | 59
Backyard Baseball | 60
Ode to My Body | 62
The Bus Home | 64
Two Windows | 65
For My City | 66
Doors and Windows | 67

IV

History | 71
Titles | 73
William James | 74
Kennedy, 1963 | 75
The Dead | 76
Wonder | 78
Catch-As-Catch-Can | 77

The End of It | 80
Smaller | 81
Doctor | 82
Listening | 83
Microfilm | 84
Shakespeare | 85
Home | 86
It Doesn't Add Up to Much | 87
It's Taken Years | 88
Esse |89
The Thing Itself | 90
In the End | 92
Memoir | 93
Do You Know What I Mean? | 94
Summer | 95
Things I Didn't Know I Loved | 96
Petrichor | 97

Acknowledgments | 99
About the Author | 101

I

Sunlight Through the Open Window

Do you have the time to pause
Here beside the open window?
To contemplate whatever you want?

I hope that's the case. I hope
You are not too stressed or
Frazzled to even see the old paint

Flaking off the window sill
And not care at all and not think
You must keep up some appearances.

So what if someone says—*He's not
Taking care of things*. We will all
Be dead soon enough. But the window

Sill will still be here—it will be—
Unpainted still. Who cares? It is
The old worn sunlight you will miss.

Because

Because I'm alive right now—
I get to say certain things—

For instance—the pine sap on
The branch yesterday—smelled

Like that island in Quetico National
Park—that floated on the border—

All those years ago. While the hot dog
I ate yesterday tasted like those ones

At *Papaya King*—East 86th Street—where I
Once was—at that corner—*where once—*

Strange

How I'm in this body
For a period of time
Yet to be determined.

Strange how you are in
Your own body at the same
Time. Strange how we are

Mostly made of moving water
Like a river or creek and we're
Here temporarily. Strange how

Despite the temporary nature
Of our presence—we know
We go beyond the life of the stars.

Strange—how all of this could be
Otherwise. How accidental—
Yet how certain our presence is.

Strange that we exist among
So many uncertainties. Even as
All of this—seems most certain.

My Blue Socks

Just now—I noticed I'm wearing
Bright blue socks—I swear

I didn't realize that until now.
Halfway through the day.

I have socks that are 40 years old—
But I don't remember these socks—

As blue as Paul Newman's eyes—
It makes me happy—*these very blue socks*

These Strange Times

The Sun is the way it's always been.
The Moon looks down with its blank face.

If you drive out into the country, away
From the city, the stars are bright and abundant.

The cats seem fine. The little gray cat chases
Her toy and brings it earnestly back. I am

Mostly fine. You are fine. The kids—fine.
But the streets are quiet. No one

At the courthouse. The mall is empty.
Is this Pompeii on a beautiful day—

August 24, 79 A.D.?—Or September 11, 2001,
Another beautiful day with a bright azure sky.

Will it be March or April or May of some unknown
Day in 2020, when we will think—*That's when*

It all changed? I try not to touch my face.
I can't help but touch your face. And my hand

Is on the door knob, the banister, the shopping
Cart. I pick up the apple, the orange, the bunch

Of bananas. I do love all the other hands before me.
I don't really care what they say. Berlin in the time

Of *Cabaret*—Jerusalem around April 7, 30 A.D.
I kiss all those hands—over and over—I kiss them.

Cars on the Freeway

The cars go by no matter what.
Everyone hurrying somewhere.

They are leaving their wives
And children. They are quitting

Their jobs—throwing the pass key
In their boss's face. But when

They arrive at the sad motel—
Of course no one is there.

Other cars are hurrying other places,
Taking others away from themselves.

Here's America. Before you sleep—pray
For our travelers— on dark and long roads.

If I Get This Wrong

It doesn't matter that much.
You will have wasted

A moment. Whereas, if I get this
Right things might really change—

For me if not for you. I might
Get someone to like this poem beside you—

And then—someone might publish it—
And then—someone else might

Want to turn this poem into a movie—
Starring—you name her or him—

And then—this poem will get an Oscar—
I'll get up on the stage and thank

Everyone responsible—including Mom
And Dad in Heaven—and even though

They will start playing the music—the music
Of my exit—I will say—*No, wait*—because

I want to thank you. Because you were there—
You were there with me before everyone else.

Sketches

I guess I've never done anything
But make these sketches on a pad.

Then I move the words around until
Something happens that transforms

Something. This is very imprecise
Because it's a sketch after all.

I don't know how to account for
Myself without this *lining*

Of my experience. It helps
That there's this regular cliff—

At the end of each line from which
I can jump—or fall—as some form

Of progress down the page.
Sometimes it's enough just to fill the line.

Other times I want some rising music or
Descending sorrow—or some coincidence

Of sound. It's just a sketch as I told you.
On a piece of lined paper. Ripped out now.

Lincoln

He gets better the more you know him.
No other American has this echoing

Presence that exists right up to now.
The photographs show a homely,

Melancholy, midwestern farm hand.
But anyone who met him said you couldn't

Really see him until he told a story—then—
His face lit up and went off into motion—

The eyebrows arching and the gray eyes
Brightening—one long leg crossed casually

Over the other—his leg dangling there as he
Arrived at the corny punchline—and looked

To you—for your reaction—which pleased him
More than anything else. His body somehow

Folded in upon itself—shyly—in the way tall people
Lessen their height to be closer to you. It's true

He loved kittens and children. He read everything
Out loud—to the annoyance of everyone around him.

His voice—high-pitched but penetrating.
His accent—*Southern* with a midwestern twang.

Like Jesus—he always had a metaphor at hand.
Tolstoy said—Lincoln wanted to be great

Through his smallness—great through his
Simplicity—a noble—through his charity.

My Mother's Babies

They did belong to her mostly—each
Of those full-term girls who died—each

One a younger sister to me. And we
Would have been seven kids—a normal

Irish-Catholic family at the time. Rather
We were a small quiet family with four

Girl ghosts who would have made me
An older brother—now I'm not anyone's

Older brother. *Margaret Mary, Mary, Jane,*
And *Mary Frances*. It seems I can't think too much—

Or imagine them too much—they are funny, beautiful
As our daughters, they love me, but I drive them nuts.

I protect them from the jerks I know. These girls—
They live in *The Land of Otherwise*—they are

Open-ended possibilities—*and wise*—they are so
Wise—they seem to know everything—

They finish my sentences—they laugh at me—
They smile—with the most beautiful smiles—

Because they know everything—and they worry
For me—because they know—I know—almost nothing.

You Told Us

You told us about an accident
You passed on the freeway on your

Way to work at the new mall.
You said the motorcycle was there

On its side. You said he was there—
(meaning the *former* motorcyclist)—

And he was obviously dead because
You saw his brains there at the edge

Of the road. And you said it was
Shocking—how his head was like

A burst flower. And it stayed with you
All day as you folded the clothes

Someone else had messed up. I wished
I could have protected you from this.

And yet—*you were so excited*—you had
That look on your face and in

Your eyes—that look I always loved.
That way your eyes brighten in a

Conspiracy of story-telling—and I'm
Sorry for the man, his family and

Friends. *But*—the story is so important
—more important than anything else.

Brooklyn Bridge

Across the room there's that long
Framed poster from the Whitney Museum
Of a drawing of the plan for the bridge

Named—*"East River Bridge"*—and from
My chair here—my perspective might be
Somewhere in New Jersey or way out

In the harbor. And in this drawing—water
Is drained from the East River and the harbor.
So we can see—in cross section—the dusky

Sand at the bed of the river and those
Planted towers. And those graceful cables
Sloping down—holding the roadway up.

Now I'm looking more closely—to see
The random sailing ship on the river.
Those unpopulated buildings on either side.

Then—there's the view from above— I never
Noticed—*God's View*—where only some
Wayward—ambitious—sea bird had ever been.

Trumpet

When I was a kid I dreamed of owning
A trumpet something about the blare

Of it the bright brilliance I thought I
Could sing with a trumpet speak with it

When I finally got a trumpet I trained
My lips carried the silver mouthpiece

In my pocket for awhile so I could play it
Then I was third trumpet of three

In high school we played the theme song
From *Alfred Hitchcock Presents* at

Basketball games then I just let my lip
Go let my fingers forget now the trumpet

Is somewhere in this house silent there
Was that time I was the first person to

Play a trumpet in the new church (now
The old church) Easter I was nervous

Behind the choir screen but the notes
Filled the church surprising and *clear*

One October Night

It's not October. It's not night.
The title is all wrong. So we're off.
The title—I just copied it from

A page in a book. A book I opened
Randomly—to find something
I could copy. If it really was—*One*

October Night—I would say it's
Surprisingly warm for October.
I would say I hate Halloween.

There it is. I always have. I might say
This particular *October Night*—it's not
So particular. It's just another one.

I might refer to the smell of dried leaves—
How we would use bed spreads to collect
All those leaves. Or Dad—he'd rake them

Into the gutter and toss his smoke—
And watch the flames rise up. I might
Invoke Death—why not bring him into it?

All of this I might do—except—it's January.
The middle of the month. A Sunday.
A gray Sunday. Absolutely not. *October*.

1957

It's 1957. Winter. I am three years old. Walking.
Sort of walking. We are at the *Catalog Counter*.
Sears on Lake Street. Minneapolis. I am bored

beyond belief, staring into the deep wood grain,
the intersecting rivers of wood grain at my eye level.
My mother is ordering something. Don't know what.

We will get it later when it doesn't matter as much
as it seems to matter to her now. She can't decide
among the shades and sizes. *Why must I wait?*

I want to return to the *Appliance Department*
where the floating beach ball spins forever, the colors
melting together above the magic vacuum.

I want to get back to the *Candy Department*—
those sprinkled chocolate stars, the corded licorice,
popcorn sounding like a snare drum in the *Sears*

Orchestra. But we're still at the *Catalog Counter*.
My mother still can't decide. She wouldn't want to make
a mistake. 1957. Winter. I walk away on my own two feet.

My First Poems

Were written on the backs
of sad check stubs—in the

MEN's room at work—West
57th Street—New York City—

in the days when you could
smoke—everywhere—and had

every occasion to smoke—
and everyone was about to be—

someone—I would be—
that one-eyed poet—who wrote—

short lines—almost Greek—
leftovers—like Sappho—they

spoke—in an absence of—
speaking—they were oddly—

enjambed—in a way no one
had ever enjambed such things—

then—when I was done with
my—*efforts*—done smoking—

done with my—*bodily needs*—
I folded my—*masterpiece*—

into that tight wad—with all
the other sad check stubs—

in my wallet—which was full
of other sad stubs of days—

like stubbed cigarettes—then—
I understood—the words came to—

nothing—and—I was silent—
for a long time—*smoking*—

carrying—*Check Stub Poems*—
a whole book of them—my own—

Harmonium—my own—*Self-Portrait
in a Convex Mirror*—unfolding them

like crumpled—*origami swans*—
still—*floating*—with music—*I heard*—

II

Us

We have this text chain *Us* it's you
Me the first kid second third but

Sometimes the kids beg off it's just
You and Me used to be the pronouns

And they know enough to not say
A thing just watch us say things

To each other that have nothing to do
With them and everything and all of it

My Parents' Wedding Album

I looked through these black and white
photographs so many times the pages are dog-
eared cracked worn over I wanted to know where
I came from so here's mother with her black
lips and her waved hair smiling with her mouth
closed she was always shy about her teeth and
father with his rimless wire glasses looks very
scholarly (he was very scholarly) but he also
seems wary as if someone might be trying to pull
something over on him and there is my father his
father his new father-in-law the best man an uncle
all of them standing backstage all of them
looking at their watches because the wedding
photographer told them to do that they seem to be
synchronizing their watches for some military
assault now and now my parents are standing
there on that *Grand Staircase* at the Boulevard
Twins on Lyndale all the wedding receptions
were held there every married couple has this
photograph the train of her bridal gown spills
down the polished stairs with a kind of elegant
excess or something like that and those stairs
are no longer there I mean in present life
they are gone just as my parents and everyone
in these photographs are not anywhere I know
just as I was somewhere else must have been why I
looked so often at this album just to *wonder* where

This

Had lunch with guys I've known for
Sixty years Dan Phil Peter we've

Known each other so long we don't
Have to say anything except every-

Thing we say leads to uncontrollable
Laughter all those old nuns in our

Background the way they tried to
Control us but we were boys pissed-

Off tacks on her chair *I don't get it
Sister—I don't know wart you mean*

Because she had a wart on her nose
We were mean and hilarious we still

Are we love each other we even say
So as we walk away to each of our cars

With Adam Zagajewski

We became friends a few emails I said
I'd take him to lunch after the reading
Take him to the airport then we drove
Around the Minneapolis lakes down
The Parkway to the intersection of
Minnehaha Parkway and Lyndale
And he turned to me and said *Do you
Know where you are?* (We happened
To be at the one place in the world
I knew best) I knew the buildings that
Were no longer there (He was antsy
About his flight) I knew the old mill
Down on the Creek a fuzzy etching
I knew *Baker's Drugs* (we called him
Old Man Baker) I knew the variety
Store called *Crossroads* the *Dairy
Queen* stand *Costello's Hardware*
(We called him *Old Man Costello)*
The barbershop where *Jerry the
Barber* let us flip through old copies
Of *Playboy* while we spun around
In his empty barber's chairs I knew
All the lost buildings the lost people
But what I said then what I said
With confidence—*I know exactly
Where I am*—and—he took it as true

All of Us

All of us are going to die how odd
We know this we still act as if

Nothing out of ordinary it's just
Ordinary except on one day for each

One of us a different day a day not
Ordinary at all it's better that it's

All of us who are headed this way
No one can take advantage the day

Will be a different day but it will
Come for each of us like a birthday

A cake the candles burning everyone
Singing that stupid song their faces

Their love did you see did you get
A piece of cake why not have another

Songs

The words come back to me
From nowhere not my brain

From vapor *Every Little Breeze*
Seems to Whisper Louise I don't

Even know the song but here it
Arrives out of air it's not even of

My generation more like something
Rudy Vallee might have sung or

Hit the Road you know the rest
It's that they come to me the words

Of old songs *Before I Put on My*
Make-Up it's that at any given time

I could be *A Lineman for the County*
Also *In South Carolina There Are*

Many Tall Pines—Jack—that was
After *Hit the Road* and I thought

The next words were *More No More*
No More No More but I think it was

No More No More No More No it's
Slightly different and did I forget

Love Potion Number Nine such a
Stupid song but I still remember it

Maria Callas

For a few years about twenty years
Ago when there was *Napster* and

The Internet was young and things
Had to come in one slow crossing

Line at a time and you paid nothing
For any music because someone took

It already I sat in the library listened
To one aria after another Maria Callas

But mostly over and over *O Mio
Babino Caro* Puccini the words mean

Oh my beloved father, etc., but who cares
About the words which are just some

Context for Maria Callas to go from
A plea to a declaration to something

Beyond love or trouble or anything
Except human longing expanded to

Flights up and down the scales from
What we abide to what we long for

A Train South

That was when we still had overt
Segregation—with separate water
Fountains at the station in Birmingham.

And I never knew Birmingham was
A center for steel. But there in early
Morning—the flames and smoke—

The stacks off to the horizon. Perhaps
They were still making dull bullets
For Lee's Army of Northern Virginia.

And all the time from Minnesota—
Clattering rails. How we walked like
Conductors—through the swaying cars.

All those miles. All the way to Florida.
Where our cousins met us. A quiet depot.
Did I say?—*Dear Aunt Phyllis*—took us.

She was born 93 years ago today.
She wanted us to have many experiences.
From which we might know the truth.

I Remember When My Mother Cried

Only a few times do I remember this
The first time in November 1963 a cold
Miserable morning when the phone
Rang so early it was odd and I only
Heard her side of the call which was
Uh huh uh huh then she pulled her
Breath into herself because her father
Had died he collapsed on the basement
Stairs and she was a little girl suddenly
So afraid and her crying scared me to
Some core of my being then another
Time June 1968 I was a paperboy and
Heard RFK had been shot way early
In our morning and I told my folks
They were still in bed and my mother
Cried the way someone cries when
Feeling overwhelms the ability to speak
It was just *Oh no, oh no, oh no, no* and
I felt bad that I was the bearer of bad
News but I learned you must just say
It when something's bad and someone
Doesn't know yet then at the end when
She was at the end we had such a nice
Visit but she had to use the bathroom
And the Jamaican nurse told us *Mother
She was crying just now* she said she
Did not want to leave and would not yet

121 East 88th Street

There we were in one room
With a tiny kitchen bathroom hall

Looking out two windows on
Robert F. Kennedy School across

The street this is where we heard
John Lennon had been killed just

Across the park we heard it below
On the street—earlier when Mohammed

Ali took out Leon Spinks in a decision all
The people the whole neighborhood

Cheered through the open windows
We had a table a couple of chairs

A convertible bed (never comfortable)
But what does anything matter if alive

I mean the guy who lived there before
Us said we should eat all our meals

In Chinatown (which he did we never)
Did do you remember the bearded

Shaggy guy with matted hair blue
Eyes he hung out at the deli he wore

A plastic tarp like Superman's cape
At night he would curl into a ball

Under the plastic he wore it like a tent
You remember him?—how long is he

Gone?—we were inside—radiators
Sputtering we were warm that's

How it's always been we were warm
No matter—as he curled into himself

Geese on the Highway

They are dumb no question
Not crows who can count

Have some self-awareness
Still Canada Geese fly south

In neat formation honk to
One another a beautiful ease

They have you can distinctly
Hear their wings overhead

Their honking so close it might
Be your own honking so close

On the highway they walk in dazed
Circles can't even decide to cross

Dumb Fucking Birds—yet I slammed
To a stop—because I know they can fly

Minnehaha Creek, 1969

Our parents mostly left us alone.
They really didn't want to know.
Everything out in the world was
Falling apart. So why shouldn't we?
We hung out every day that summer
At the Dupont Bridge. A WPA project
From the Depression. We knew shit
About the Depression. That's what
We said about everything. *I know
Shit*. About whatever. We smoked
Cigarettes. Actually we stole them
From the dairy store up on Lyndale.
That poor man—*Bob*—who owned
The store. We tormented him.
He probably gave his life to annoyance
Over us. We kissed the girls. The girls
Were right there with us. The girls
Were so something else. We didn't
Know what to do. We would swim in
That warm summer water of the Creek.
It would surround us. It would carry
Us in a slow procession toward the great
Mississippi. We knew we only lived on
This small tributary. We knew larger
Forces were at work. Sliding down
The continent. We'd catch crayfish.
We'd light firecrackers inside tin cans.
Generally, we were about disturbance.
Our long hair. Those goofy flared jeans.
It took only a few years to change from
All that. Now Minnehaha Creek. Just

A creek. Running through the city.
Once it was wild. Flooding its banks
Each spring. Icing solid in winter.
What we knew—*Laughing Water*.
The *haha* part. We knew that well.

Steelhead Trout

I get this stunning fillet from Costco
Peel back the plastic wrap rinse this
Slab of fish under cold water slice it
Into about six or seven portions for
Six or seven meals in my life *my life*
With asparagus or mashed potatoes
Or sliced tomato with mozzarella and
I take out a frozen portion from the
Freezer let it rest for awhile in the
Refrigerator then on a plate on the
Counter and I *strew* salt we have
From the store in Paris Julia Child
Loved that's called *Sel de Camargue*
Salt marshes on the Mediterranean
The Sun the way the Suns sees it all
Salt supposedly *harvested by hand*
All I can say is *Bien* because the salt
This salt on the fillet changes the
Flesh of the fish as if the fish can
Return to its sea then in the oven how
This *pink* flesh changes to an older
Form of pink more *salmon* in color
Steelhead Trout much like salmon
But better in its own way *gamier*
(I might just be imagining this)
(What can I do but imagine?) I mean
Considering I do have to eat to keep
Going in this life *my life* shouldn't
I say this poem for the fish I will eat?

Morton Man Dies in ATV Crash in Renville County

First of all it's not me I would never be on
An ATV plus I'm not a Morton man
I have no idea where Morton is moreover

I'm pretty sure I've never been to Renville
County wherever that is but even if I had
I wouldn't ever be on an ATV what a silly

Way to die I mean *He died in an ATV
Accident* might as well say he was a total
Douchebag or something worse I can't

Say but it's really not at all good and it
Shouldn't matter how you die heart cancer
Some total stroke or auto immune thing

But you should try not to be that Morton
Man on an ATV flying off the narrow path
Into the trees the deepest part of the woods

Oyster Shells

I've just eaten six of these creatures.
In their salty brine. And now—

The shells sit here before me. Propped up
In a bed of ice. These are the places

Pearls grow. Around a speck of sand.
These are the milky walls to which

The creature attaches itself. I'm assuming
The creature has a self to attach. The outside

Of the shell is as rough as the Himalayas.
You've seen those paths. The difficult way up.

While inside—*well the inside*—it is this
Surprising crèche where Mary holds her son.

You know how she looks down on him.
She will never take her eyes off of him.

So these are oyster shells before me.
It's what I told you. Sturdy and beautiful houses.

They make me believe. Nothing is ever forgotten.
What's thrown away is most beautiful.

III

I Like Room Service

This—I'm not proud of—
I don't like—tents—hikes—

Canoes—backpacks—mosquito
Netting—anything canned—

Dehydrated—to be mixed
With water—anything that

Has to be earned through
Some unusual physical effort.

Basically—I like room service.
Here I am lying on the bed

And you bring me a cheeseburger
And a pretty good chocolate

Malt—and the French fries are OK.
And you bring all of this to me

On a clattering cart—and you lift
The silver dome to present—

Cheeseburger and fries with a sick pickle
And wilted lettuce. But it's—

Room Service—so everything's—
For the most part—forgiven.

When

That was when we were really something
It was some time after we arrived

But before we left I remember thinking
How extraordinary—this life

We lived above the river this was
Many years after they stopped

The ferry service but many years before
They began it again the old wind

Off the river was as it's always been
The wind had a way of clearing our minds

Some days we just sat on the stoop
To watch it all before us remember that

How it seemed we were floating
The wind shifting from here to there

Scam Likely

I think it's so forthright of them
To announce themselves on my phone
As *Scam Likely*. I almost want to

Pick up the call and say—*Thank you
For being upfront about your intentions.*
But I don't do that and *Scam Likely*

Goes into the ether—looking for some
Sucker other than me. Calling numbers
Endlessly. It must be a tough life

For *Scam Likely*. First of all—he—
(Why is he a he?)—should change
His name from—*Scam Likely*—

To—*Bob Olsen*. I would probably
Answer a call from *Bob Olsen*—
Figuring he might be some insurance

Agent. Or some death benefit
Cremation Society guy I could put off.
And yet—*Scam Likely*—he is what

He is. He has to be himself. He's
From a long line of *Likelies*—
His father was a—*Scam*—his father too.

The Sweetness of Water

On long summer days after mowing
The lawn or cleaning the fogged windows—

On days when the sun beats down and
I find myself sweating like a butcher—

I drink a whole tall glass of water and my
Head clears and I'm brought back to

Some kind of equilibrium—as if the water
Of my body needed some kind of ballast

From water outside my body—and that water—
At those times—it's so sweet—like the first

Idea of water—that water doesn't even have to be
Cold—it can be room temperature—and it brings

Me back to the room I find myself in—it brings me
Back to the room of myself.

I bet you understand this as I say it—
We are intersecting fresh water *locales* connected

One-to-another by those cold rushing streams
And those long—sometimes difficult—*portages*.

For Where You Used to Live

All those rooms and doorknobs and windowsills.
The particular dance you made at the front door,
pulling and pushing at once as the key turned
and you walked in—surprisingly—on yourself.
Those corners filled with dust. Appliances that broke
or worked perfectly but hummed like a familiar pet.
That galley kitchen along the narrow brick corridor
with a combination sink/refrigerator/stove, as if
you were playing *House*, with ice cubes melting,
dinner cold, the dishes piled up. Then those neighbors—
close as siblings in their time—they
became distant. Lost cousins. Dead. Divorced.
The familiarity of a phone number, zip code, almost
as close as your name. The route home you decided to
take that day to find yourself again inside your rooms as
in your body. The rooms being an extension
of your body in time and place. All that looking out from
where you were. All that yearning for the future and the
desire to be in the place you were meant, now and then
being as good as anything. Located as you
were—above the bakery, beside the river, across from a
brick wall, with a vision of a deli, animal hospital,
a drugstore, the QE2 arrived back from the Falklands,
the Methodist Church, a hedge, a wall of snow. How
you walked surely—as the blind do—through your own
dark rooms. Your hand on the wall, banister, doorknob.
Knowing where to turn, stop, rise up, fall down, most
definitely, knowing how to pull the switch, to find
the light. To find yourself again in the cloudy mirror.

Aramaic Galilean Accent

I can pull my phone out of my pocket
Punch a few keys with my thumb and

Listen and watch as a serious man speaks
The Lord's Prayer in Aramaic with a

Galilean accent which is the way Jesus
Spoke and they say that the Galilean

Accent was harsh and anyone in Jerusalem
Would know the speaker was Galilean

From the wild north a hick a nobody some
Things never change although I think

In the distant dark future who could ever
Believe you might listen to a ghost speak

In his own voice and accent his own words
And that you could rewind to listen again

Crickets

I miss them in winter—
Crickets—they were so
Comforting in late August.

Their regular song
Is the song of dusk.
The song of falling away.

The song of *nonetheless*.
When the dishes are done
But you can't go to bed.

They sing all night from
The bushes near the house.
They cause windows to open.

Where do they go in winter?
Are they sad without their song?
Or simply dead? It's just that—

I'm slayed by the song of crickets.
Sweet. *Jangly*. Bells at the edge.
While night falls all around.

Backyard Baseball

Three white plastic chairs
are first, second and third.
My empty wallet is home plate.
Frankie waits patiently on first.

His legs dangle from the chair.
He grows as he waits.
Maeve chokes up on the bulbous
green bat. She is sly beyond

her years. She giggles as I pitch.
Of course it's a hit.
First and second. No outs.
Elizabeth eyes me with suspicion.

She would believe in Santa Claus
if it made enough sense.
Fat and wobbly pitch.
Dished right over the plate.

She tries too hard to hit.
Spins herself around.
Makes herself fall, laughing.
Now she resets. Waits

Definite single to me.
I can't run them down.
Why would I? *Let it be*
An endless inning.

Stranded at their corners.
The sky remains blue—that blue
from the roof of heaven
where we've arrived.

Ode to My Body

Suit of shadows. Close
echo. Strange cousin.
Snoring head. Receding
hairline. Widening nose.
Big ears. Small cock.
Would like to think—
noble forehead, big cock,
big heart. Sometimes.
Blue eyes. Gray eyes really.
Sweaty feet. Bag of bones.
Body bag. Articulate
platform. Mid-aged.
If one lives to be 100.
Caboose of the train.
Locomotive of the train.
Sometimes the track.
Sometimes the ditch.
A continent of skin shed.
Zoo of the gut. Host
of Asian flu. Smashed finger.
Not temple of the soul.
Maybe diner of the soul.
Or bowling alley of the soul.
Transporter. Transformer.
Walker. Picker upper. Washer.
Then hair—straight and curly,
gray and brown. White.
Out of the nose. Out of
the ears. On the nape
of the neck. Dear heart.
Sweet kidneys. Oblivious liver.

Placid testicles. Mysterious
hypothalamus gland. Water
in. Water out. Seminal
vesicles. Tibular something.
Soon the rash. Now
the embarrassment. Later
a broken hip. Something
that can't be heard.
Trick knee. Sunburn.
Stab wound. A fight
over a woman. Scars.
Nipple this. Aorta that.
Left lung. Right nostril.
Anus. Iris. Mucus. Heel.
Deep veins. Worn knuckles.
Long legs. Looking down
their length to the floor,
the grass, the sand.
Clear eyes now. Clear
eyes looking out now.

The Bus Home

For me it was the 18-G
which started downtown
on Nicollet and ended up
at Southdale or the airport

But it dropped me off
just beyond Minnehaha Creek
near Thompson Lumber
and Bill's Shoe Repair

Near the sign that spelled
M-O-T-E-L in humming
downward sequence
just as the night came on

And I had a home
with parents who let me be
and a brother and sister
I could get to laugh

And a dog—*there must always
be a dog*—Kip—who loved me—
his eyes gazing into mine—
from a very close distance.

Two Windows

In an old room looking South.
I've been here before—

on East 88th Street, on East
9th Street, now on West

Franklin Avenue. I'm much
older now, although if I stop

whatever I am doing, listen
to the traffic, watch the late sunlight

falling on red brick across the street,
I remember completely the close

anxiety of youth, the busyness of my
one mind then. Now I know I'm

of many minds, the least of which
seems to belong only to me.

For My City

I love that we are at the edge of everything—
the edge of the prairie, the edge of winter,
on the lee-side of a summer storm,
in the track of tornados. I love that we
are looped around with lakes and roll along
the river. Even the foot path beside
the creek makes me feel marginal.

I love that we are land-locked, without
an obvious port. When the wind rises,
it brings the farm smells—fresh corn
from a field, a skunk stopped on hot asphalt.
All the rich earth. I love that we built
these hunkered down bungalows,
and Tudor stucco semi-cathedrals, and sometimes

Spanish tiled fortresses—*so odd*—surrounded
by snow. Once, we were all dusted in flour
by Pillsbury and Robin Hood, and the smells then
from the bread factories and the linseed oil
refineries made us believe the Earth
was close, and we were part of a great
harvest, floating downriver in slow barges.

My city of rolling sidewalks, built up
above the river, as if to ignore the river.
But we couldn't ignore that ancient sturgeon,
hundreds of years old. He made his way
to compact Lake Harriet, in the heart of my city.
All the grizzled years from which he escaped.
By crawling across limestone to find water.

Doors and Windows

These habits of unlatching, unlocking, turning
the porcelain knob, lifting the squeaky sash, pulling
the past gently behind you to seal it off in the room,

raising the clackety blinds to look out through all your eyes,
listening for the slam of the car door out on the street,
pushing the electric button, feeling the full wind,

lapping the air like water rushing by on the highway,
being a retriever of the hello and goodbye, accomplishing
these constant daily transformations, crossing

the threshold again and again, coming in and going out,
until you become—*all threshold*— your face being the site
of all the thresholds you've crossed, into all the rooms,

out of all the houses, with that surprise, weariness, that leap
of love, the turning of the key, the leaning on the sill,
the dancing on the threshold, the door in your arms.

IV

History

It's a candle in the corner of the room.

It's an amphora of olive oil on the sea bed.

It's the paper advertising corsets and liniment.

It's a petrified log tight with stony rings.

It's Yorick's skull and the little bell jangling inside.

It's the sound of sand dropping on a glass eye.

It's the mildew in the basement.

It's the dungeon where someone slowly died.

It's the wind rushing through the broken wall.

It's the drum at the pow wow and those voices rising.

It's the lapping of the lake.

It's the circling of the birds.

It's the peace after the One-Hundred Year War.

It's the graveyard. It's the moss.

It's the copper tablet. It's the quote.

It's the voices singing or screaming or praying.

It's the laugh track, the scratched record.

It's the rusty tin can, the compost heap.

It's the sweet worms. It's the voices.

It's the candle—*flickering*—in the corner of the room.

Titles

I keep lists of them to hold
a moment—*Leaves. Light in the Afternoon.*

Remember When. Sometimes they are the first words.
Or the last. Or not said at all

except here in capitals above. Either
The Heart of the Matter or *Suppressed Speech.*

How about *A Summing Up?* How about
The Pear? If the title doesn't work,

the rest will be sad and shapeless.
Sad, Shapeless and Not Music.

I keep these little wooden boxes
each labeled with its title.

They will grow or not. Surviving
only on *Leaves and Grass* in the dark.

Any of them could rise up one day
and send me off. *The Light Fantastic.*

Into *A Reverie.* Or cause me to *Sleep in the Afternoon.*
So many possibilities. *So Many*

Possibilities! With the years going by.
The Years....Before They Come Back.

William James

Speaking
        on the possibility
                of human immortality

he gently unwound
        two premises—

                a) the death of the brain
                      is the death of the soul; and

                b) there can never be
                      enough rooms in Heaven
                          to accommodate the
Chinese
                            let alone us.

With respect to a)—
        he wondered whether
                there are other worlds
                      we cannot see
                          from our platforms.

On b)—
        he determined
                our imaginations can
                      take in the whole world
                          including Heaven
                            and all
                                its many
rooms.

Kennedy, 1963

That was when it all began—
*The dread—*The—*I Suppose This*

Won't Work Out. The obvious
Fix was in for anything that

Might remotely inspire us. So
We became cynical. I should say

I became cynical— at nine-years-old.
It was that Sunday morning when Oswald

Was shot in the gut on the TV screen.
How many times did he flinch that day?

As the old fashioned hat of Jack Ruby
And his snub nose pistol moved in?

I remember how his face was only pain.
So much pain in his face— it became ours.

In those few days we came to believe
Oswald did it. Probably alone. Probably

Just because. We always make people
Crazy. We are very good at that.

The Dead

When someone dies—all their loved ones—
go through days of static noise—

like scrambled radio messages from
the Middle East—there's the echo

of his voice—the reverberation of the way
she brushed back her hair—and so the dead

are very active in those few days—
using us as instruments for what

they didn't say—or were unable to do—
or could not imagine—and then—there's that

sense of—a waste of words—that the dead
will never say anything again—not with any

dental snap or belly laugh—not with the resonance
of the body's chamber—and then it comes—

when the days go long with silence—
as if the dead one was simply being—

obstinate—or—*coy*—or was waiting to hear
the words of ours that might come to our minds—

those memories of the water and the sky—
the house at the end of the block—the room—

then come the nights—when the dead slip through
the velvet curtain—to stand on the stage

of our dreams—where we put an unlikely wig
on her head—or dress him like Julius Caesar—

and the dead are the best actors in the cast—
by far—they are so convincing in the characters

we've created for them—*the characters*—we have
yet to be—but sense—*there's*—the grief of it all.

Wonder

What will they make of us in the future
when they sift through our debris, when they
apply their speculative minds to us?

Will they think—"I've found the key to the lexicon
in this *Chock Full O' Nuts* coffee can." Or—
"Rituals were conducted at *Airports* facing southwest."

Will they imagine our royal processions in wooden cars
across *I-80* in Nebraska? Will they search
for a *Ford Fairlaine*, having found the repair book?

Surely they will find our bones and skulls—no
surprises there. But how will they understand that
8-track tape of *Blood, Sweat & Tears,* how

to hear that voice, the jabbing brass section, wind
rushing past with the highway rushing past, that
deep sense of freedom? Maybe the TV, radio, micro

waves will bounce forever between canyon walls
in Syria—waiting to be caught by a *sensitive device.*
Maybe our heartbeats will be monitored remotely

eons later—had we lived this is how our hearts
would sound—that old song of the heartbeat—
pitched to the inner ear—coincident with the moon.

Catch-As-Catch-Can

When you could smoke in bathrooms
or anywhere I would write poems

on the backs of check stubs—long narrow
poems like Creeley I thought—by way

of Dr. Williams—who wrote poems on prescription
pads between office visits or at the side of a road.

I have no desk, no quill pen, no creamy paper,
no mood music or incense. I have no examples

that I carry in memory. Just me—and a Bic pen—
might as well be a Sienna Crayon where I

rip the paper to get down to the nub—might as well
be that yellow paper full of woodchips

we used in grade school—and we tried to stay
within those blue lines—some dotted some solid—

the flourishes of our handwriting being too precise.
I have no message or concept—no ulterior motive—

no elevator speech. I would like to build a moat
around the possibilities of a panel discussion or

bury my intentions in smoke, float them in the warm
bathtub water, excise them from a glossy circular.

It's simple—I have always wanted this to be *now*—
with you beside me each breath of the way.

The End of It

After my uncle died after we went
Through the attic basement the nooks

Where my grandpa stashed pints of
Old Crow Whiskey after the letters

And photographs and pots and pans
After the tools encyclopedias and all

The *what not* all the *this and that* all
The playing cards watches tooth

Brushes and sharpened pencils I sat
In the sunroom waiting for the van

That would take what was left take it
Nowhere you know I wept right there

Smaller

My doctor says—"We generally
want to get smaller
as we get older."

He says this because I'm
getting bigger which is not
the right direction.

I thought to ask him—
"How small?" I thought that
would be impertinent.

Small enough to land
on the head of a pin? Small
enough to fit between tweezers?

As small as one needs to be.
My doctor's voice is getting
smaller now so he sounds

like he's way across the bay
whispering into his wife's ear
something he never said before.

Doctor

My heart doctor has a bunch
Of statistics on how many kids

From private schools in Minnesota
Make it into Harvard—and I'm quite

Mildly interested—but what does
Any of this have to do with

My heart? My heart does not
Care at all about entrance exams.

My heart wants that smoke you
Owe me. My heart is more interested

In my soul—which really doesn't give
A shit about any of this. I can't say

Any of this (shit) to the heart doctor—
Who stares into the black and white

Scan and sees predictions and likelihoods.
There are possibilities that translate into

Nothing. Turns out—I know a great deal about
Nothing—turns out—it's my area of expertise.

Listening

I learned about listening
from my grandmother Ruth

who allowed great silences
to live and breathe

in a conversation. She
then would say the most

apt thing, having thought
about what she would say.

And then she would return
to quiet. She knew the give

and take—and she knew—
most of it should be give—

Microfilm

*"I crammed my head full of as much of this stuff as I could
stand and locked it away in my mind out of sight, let it alone."*

– Bob Dylan, *Chronicles: Vol. 1*

At the New York Public Library, the lions preside every day
whether the day begins in fog or sleet or a pile of snow.
In the microfilm cubby, on a wobbly table, he spun the film

through those shiny sprockets, paused on medicinal remedies,
the news from Fort Sumter, the call-up of recruits. The day
he was in didn't matter too much. He slept in someone's

apartment, listened to records, read a French poet, drank
coffee with sugar and cream. The day that mattered was
long ago. He was trying to hear the music of that day through

the news of that day, the songs they played at Dodsworth's
Dancing Academy in Brooklyn, the melody of Professor Wood's
Hair Restorative, the simple American sense of Winslow's

Soothing Syrup, for teething children, impressive testimonials.
You never can know what you might need, a phrase, a turn,
an odd coincidence. The words come into focus when you turn

the black knob. The important thing—to lock it away,
let it alone, being certain it will all come back again.

Shakespeare

He was a poor philosopher—
an abrupt battle coordinator—
he cribbed old plots—set everything

in some imagined Italy—then made
bouquets of flowers—flowers
made of sounds—they banked

the country lanes—he dropped
the mechanics and day laborers
in at odd intervals—to set off the royals—

to put them in some perspective—
he joyfully accepted our variety—
and let the least of his characters

speak as a poet in this new English—
he must have been a great actor—
unacknowledged—knowing how

each player would sound—
as Hamlet or Macbeth—if they trusted
his words—they would arrive—

like Caliban—sucked along
by the Gulf Stream—washed ashore
at the mouth of the Thames.

Home

So I always knew these rooms would be here,
these small closets, the close nooks and corners.

So I knew I would open this door and breathe
deeply in and see the floor plan of the future—

down the hall to the right or to the left. So
I knew I would be within these shingles and studs,

looking out this clear glass into the yard, to the sky
which goes on being blue and bright. The trees

are just leafing out. I knew it would be this way.

It Doesn't Add Up to Much

When I was a young man
my father said—*It doesn't add up
to much*—that was the day
his father died—he said this
in one of those interval
moments—as we drove from
the funeral home—one of those
stark moments—when the sky
nonetheless remains blue.

Then—I saw his face for the first time—
and let him be a stranger as I watched.
I was surprised he would tell me
It doesn't add up to much—since
that seemed a burden and not a gift.
And I was used to gifts. Now
I realize—*It doesn't add up to much*—
expands—just as it seems
to swallow itself.

It's Taken Years

It's taken years for me to get back
to where I was that early evening

early spring when I was six-years old
and left my family inside while I

went outside into the front yard
the grass just beginning to sprout

the earth still deeply cold from winter
and I laid myself down in my small presence

in my narrow grave with the great sky
above me and all the stars I could not name

turning above me as part of an elaborate
master clock. I understood that the stars

were displayed just for me—the *me* I was
at that moment. Now I am a vague cousin

to that boy—familiar around the eyes—
tending toward the same humor.

How have I survived all these years?
The night was getting cold. Nobody noticed

when I came back in. The warm and close light.
My mother at the sink. My dad with his paper.

I could not possibly explain to them how far
 had traveled or how long I had been away.

Esse

Do you have the sense that if things worked out
the way you want them to, you would still
not be satisfied? Do you think this is the secret

you carry with you like a single amulet in a leather bag?
Why not honor dissatisfaction, construct a memorial
to it among the ruins? You could have your very own

Roman Forum, with the wreckage of the Temple of Venus,
your own lost lives imagined there on the Coliseum floor.
You might recount all those mistaken votes in the Senate.

Who can forget the many assassinations when you
played the parts of both Brutus and Caesar?
Here, in this very place, you first entered the City.

A group resembling your family waited here for you.
In this place, you spoke eloquently for some cause
you cannot remember now. You've forgotten your words.

Here you christened your children or paused at night
to follow the constellations as they tumbled above you.
You wanted to name each of the heroes and horses.

This magic dust. These complex weeds. Such fateful stones.
You have the sense that the other side of what you know
looks and smells just like this—the warm and jumbled marble,

the scattered limbs, a Greek amphora filled with olive oil.
You were struck in particular by all those troops returning
from their lost wars. Each on their own path up from the sea.

The Thing Itself

If you shove it off the edge of the table,
it will break like an egg, a plate,
a water glass. If you bend it, it will

lean toward the ocean, the sunrise, the path.
If you divert it, it will come back
another way, in another form, such as

ice, liquid, vapor. When you speak sternly,
it will avoid you. When you speak softly,
it will turn its belly up. It is a mirror,

a body of water, a leaf. It sings,
when you listen. It weeps from the other room.
You work on it, to turn it from stone to flesh.

When you speak its language, you
stumble with the grammar and the tense.
It has no tense. You possess the tense.

You need to have it around you
on the desk, the end table, on the counter.
It is the semblance of you moving

through the world, in your day, in your own
morning. It is the dew on the grass,
the ashes in the pit, the family bones

in the corner. It can be the grease
in the pan, the lost button, the license plate
nailed up in the garage. It always works

on you with no discernable effort, always works
to catch your attention. You suppose
it has always been this way. Always will be.

Passive and loud at once, it is mowed, caressed,
caught, pushed, carried. When it falls from the window
high above, it falls with your exact weight.

In the End

What a mess we're in don't remember
Anything like this ever in my life

All screwed up it's all wrecked we
Stand in the wreckage soon enough

We won't be able to stand we've
Brought everything down around us

Nothing really works sure the birds
And trees will survive us but we've

Taken too much space in the whole
Scheme of things we are totally too

Much I just saw a chipmunk scurry
Across the driveway away from me

My lumbering car the garage door
Rising all I can think of is the chip-

Munk's tiny heart the vastness of it
The way he looks here then there

Memoir

There were days when I was worried—mostly about money
sometimes about love. Days when the sun lit the snow
and I thought I would burst with the joy of the cold. Days
of brilliant blue skies and soft casual rain. Days travelling
across the country during a heat wave racing above
a soft road. Day-in/day-out days when nothing special
happened—when I just barely survived—when I was
full of possibilities. Summer days in New York City—
a kid dancing by with a boom box booming. Days of death.
The days when the kids were born. A day devoted
to an old friend. Thanksgiving Days and Christmas Days
and Good Fridays when life seemed on a pivot point.
Those perpetual days of summer as a kid—down at the lake
for the whole day. Not-so-special and very special days.
Days made for no good. Days made of only good.
Sacramental days along with those birthdays and death days
that seemed to mark some passage, as if from here on out
it would all be different. A couple of days in Paris.
I wandered around by myself. I stopped when I wanted.
I sat down at a café table. It seemed endless, for the moment,
the days would go on and would always somehow involve me.

Do You Know What I Mean?

As you wake up—all the little nothings
are released from your dream

like a flock of monarchs—they
hardly bend the blades of grass—

and—the mongrel armies gather forces—
as you bathe and shave—your nose

broadens—and your eyes—*oh*—what
tender shock in seeing them again.

How did you select this costume
of your body from all the possibilities?

And each gathering moment presents
a question you would like to avoid.

I know you know what I mean—
this lightness of the self—this

transparent veil—it covers your face
in sorrow or in joy—sometimes—

in those brief moments—
you understand all the lively accidents.

Summer

Once I get started, you'll know
what I mean. It's when the cool

winds come down from Canada
and the crickets wake up

as the sun goes down. You've
eaten a tomato and the juice

dribbles down your chin. If
you are beside a body of water,

looking out, you will feel,
for the moment, that you have no

skin, that the water you look out on
is the composition of you. And the sun

leaving its grand throne, is your
abdication. Then the night

surrounds you. The trees breathe in
and out. You think: *Here*

right now: eternity on a pin.
The grass is still green. Radiant

beside the blacktop. Once I
conclude, you'll know what I mean.

We are moving. With the children.
Hesitant. Coming home in the dark.

Things I Didn't Know I Loved

after Nazim Hikmet

It's November 2020. I'm sitting
At a high-top table amidst
A pandemic in a hotel coffee bar.

On the West Bank of the Mississippi.
Minneapolis. I just read the local
Newspaper. The Vikings beat

The Packers. I don't care one bit.
What I didn't know I loved—
The Mississippi River. How it's always

Been in my life. Sometimes rushing by
As cold water from snow melt up North.
Sometimes *lolling*—in slow procession

Pulling me to the South and gentler lands.
I didn't know I loved the trees that bank
The river—the elms and oaks—

The birches and scrub pines. Especially
I didn't know I loved the saplings
Clinging so earnestly to the rock shelf

Above the river. I didn't know I loved
The rock shelf. Set this way since
The Ice Age. I didn't know I loved

The Ice Age. Or any age for that matter.
Especially *The Age of Now*. Which
I didn't know I loved. *This very now*.

Petrichor

The smell of rain on concrete
Or asphalt that smell you know

When you stand at the side
Of an old country road the rain

Has just stopped the Sun about to
Come out and you breathe in

Petrichor named by researchers
In Australia in the 1960s who found

The smell was produced by bacteria
The molecule named *Geosmin*

The bacteria named *Streptomyces*
The researchers named Isabel Bear

And RG Thomas they named it
The smell *Petrichor* from the Greek

Petros—"stone" the Greek *Ichor*—
"Fluid that flows in the veins of gods"

Don't you see the perfect sense
Standing there at the side of the road

The Sun on your face knowing
You are a god where you stand

Acknowledgments

Common Good Books: "It Doesn't Add Up to Much." Contest Winner, 2017.

Great River Review: "Kennedy, 1963," and "Things I Didn't Know I Loved."

Minnesota Family Housing Fund: "Home."

Legal Studies Forum: "The Dead," "Do You Know What I Mean?," "Doors and Windows," "Esse," "The Journey," "My First Poems," "William James," and "Wonder."

Mudfish: "Memoir," "My Mother's Babies," "My Parents' Wedding Album," "Ode to My Body," "Oyster Shells," and "Smaller."

17th Mudfish Poetry Prize, 2023: "Memoir."

New Rivers Press: Visiting Bob: Poems Inspired by the Life and Work of Bob Dylan: "Microfilm."

Poetry Ireland Review: "Two Windows."

Sports Literate: "Backyard Baseball."

Saint Paul Almanac: Impression: "Listening."

Troubadour Poetry Contest, London: "1957."

Tim Nolan was born in Minneapolis, graduated from the University of Minnesota with a B.A. in English, and from Columbia University in New York City with an M.F.A. in writing. Tim is an attorney in private practice in Minneapolis. His poems have appeared in *The Gettysburg Review, The Nation, The New Republic, Ploughshares*, and on *The Writer's Almanac* and *American Life in Poetry*. His first three collections—*The Sound of It, And Then,* and *The Field,* were published by New Rivers Press. His most recent collection, *Lines*, was published by Nodin Press. He is the host of the series *Readings by Writers* at the University Club in St. Paul.